I0417282

# Ways to Wear Silk Scarves

CANDICE HELD

Copyright © 2017 Candice Held Studio

All rights reserved.

ISBN:1544648707
ISBN-13:9781544648705

# DEDICATION

This book is dedicated to my mother, Karen Held,
my grandmother, Claudie Stant, and my
great-grandmother, Mimi Dhainault.

# WAYS TO WEAR SILK SCARVES

# CONTENTS

Acknowledgments i

1 The Starlet Pg 1

2 The Jet Setter Pg 2

3 The Outlaw Pg 3

4 The Lady Pg 4

5 The Flirt Pg 5

6 The Butterfly Pg 6

7 The Beach Bunny Pg 7

8 The Fashionista Pg 8

9 The Rocker Pg 9

10 The Flight Attendant Pg 10

11 The Ingenue Pg 11

12 The Flashback Pg 12

13 The Flapper Pg 13

14 The Bohemian Pg 14

15 The Influencer Pg 15

# ACKNOWLEDGMENTS

Cover photo by Brandise Daneswich

Illustrations by Candice Held

# 1
# THE STARLET

### Large Square Scarf

Fold a large square scarf in half into a triangle, matching corner to corner.
Place on head with center of long edge at forehead, triangle point towards the back of head.
Wrap long edge around face.
Cross ends in front of neck under chin, wrap around to the back of neck, and tie at nape of neck.
Alternatively, simply knot ends loosely under chin without wrapping to back.

# 2
# THE JET SETTER

### Large Square Scarf

Fold a large square scarf in half into a triangle, matching corner to corner.

Place on head with center of long edge at forehead, triangle point towards the back of head.

Wrap long edge around crown of head towards back, over point end of triangle.

Knot ends securely at back of head.

# 3
# THE OUTLAW

## Large Square Scarf

Fold a large square scarf in half into a triangle, matching corner to corner.
Place center of long edge under chin, triangle pointing down toward waist.
Wrap around to the back of neck, cross ends, and bring back around to knot in front.

# 4
# THE LADY

## Large Square Scarf

Fold lengthwise in half (edge to edge), then into quarters.
Place center at back of neck.
Bring ends around to front.
Bring one end under the other.
Pull through to sit on top.

Otherwise known as The Ascot.

# 5
# THE FLIRT

### Large Square Scarf

Fold a large square scarf in half into a triangle, matching corner to corner.
Place center of long edge at back between shoulder blades, triangle pointing down toward waist.
Bring ends around shoulders to tie in front at chest.

# 6
# THE BUTTERFLY

## Large Square Scarf

Fold in half lengthwise, right sides together.
Knot corners together on each side.
Turn right side out.
Put arms through openings, knotted corners at front.

# 7
# THE BEACH BUNNY

### Large Square Scarf

Fold a large square scarf in half into a triangle, matching corner to corner.
Place center of long edge at chest over bust, triangle pointing down toward waist.
Wrapping tightly over bust, bring ends around to the back and tie in a secure square knot.

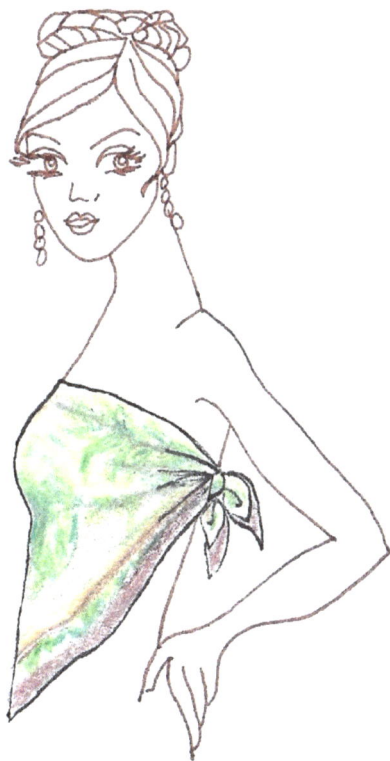

# 8
# THE FASHIONISTA

### Oblong or Bias Scarf

Fold scarf in half, thirds, or quarters lengthwise, depending on desired width. If scarf is narrow, do not fold.
Place center of long edge at front of neck.
Wrap around to the back of neck, cross ends, and bring back around to hang loosely in front.

# 9
# THE ROCKER

### Oblong or Bias Scarf

Fold scarf in half, thirds, or quarters lengthwise, depending on desired width. If scarf is narrow, do not fold.
Place center of long edge at back of neck.
Bring ends around to the front, hanging one end longer.
Tie a loose simple knot in the longer end.
Bring the shorter end into and through the knot.
Tighten to desired length.

# 10
# THE FLIGHT ATTENDANT

### Oblong or Bias Scarf

Fold scarf in half, thirds, or quarters lengthwise, depending on desired width. If scarf is narrow, do not fold.
Place center of long edge at back of neck.
Bring ends around to the front, hanging one end longer.
Tie a loose simple bow at clavicle, pulling loops long.

# 11
# THE INGENUE

### Oblong or Bias Scarf

Fold scarf in half, thirds, or quarters lengthwise, depending on desired width. If scarf is narrow, do not fold.
Pull hair into loose, low ponytail and secure with elastic band.
Place center of long edge at top of elastic.
Wrap scarf around elastic.
Tie a loose simple bow around ponytail, covering elastic.

# 12
# THE FLASHBACK

Oblong or Bias Scarf

Fold scarf in half, thirds, or quarters lengthwise, depending on desired width. If scarf is narrow, do not fold.
Place center of scarf at front of hairline.
Wrap ends around to nape of neck, over tops of ears and under hair.
Tie at nape of neck in square knot, slightly off center.
Bring long ends to front.

# 13
# THE FLAPPER

### Oblong or Bias Scarf

Fold scarf in half, thirds, or quarters lengthwise, depending on desired width. If scarf is narrow, do not fold.
Place center of scarf at temple, off center to one side.
Wrap ends around to back of head, over tops of ears.
Bring around to opposite side, off center, and tie in simple bow.

# 14
# THE BOHEMIAN

## Oblong or Bias Scarf

Fold scarf in half, thirds, or quarters lengthwise, depending on desired width. If scarf is narrow, do not fold.
Place center of scarf at temple, off center to one side.
Wrap ends around to back of head, over tops of ears.
Bring around to opposite side, off center, and tie in square knot.
Leave ends to hang loose.

# 15
# THE INFLUENCER

Oblong or Bias Scarf

Fold scarf in half, thirds, or quarters lengthwise, depending on desired width. If scarf is narrow, do not fold.
Place center of scarf at underside of wrist.
Wrap ends around wrist.
Continue wrapping until ends are short.
Tie in simple knot.

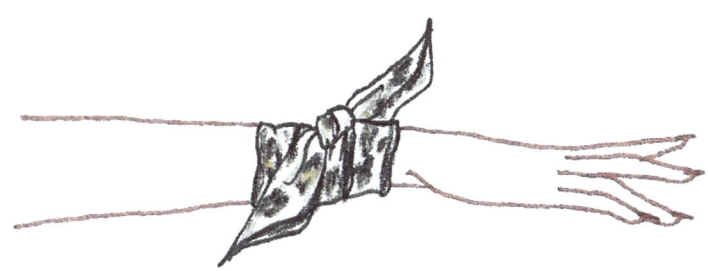

# ABOUT THE AUTHOR

Candice Held designs original textile prints for her eponymous fashion line, silk scarves, and home décor products including wallpaper and home textiles.

Candice became known in 2004 for her unique and original one-of-a-kind dresses made from recycled vintage scarves. Working with so many prints and colors while designing her vintage line inspired Candice to begin designing her own textile prints.

Many celebrities have been photographed in original Candice Held dresses, including Beyoncé, Paris Hilton, Halle Berry, Britney Spears, Drew Barrymore, Carmen Electra, Christina Applegate, Maria Sharapova, and Tyra Banks. Tyra featured Candice on her "Top 5 Hottest Designers to Watch" show in 2006.

In addition to designing for her own line, she has also designed textile prints for companies such as Equipment, Rachel Zoe, and Kenneth Jay Lane Scarves.

Candice lives in Palm Springs, CA with her husband, Tristan Gittens.

Candice's designs can be found at her two boutiques (in Palm Desert, CA on El Paseo Drive and at The Shops at Thirteen Forty Five in Palm Springs), or online at www.candiceheld.com

www.ingramcontent.com/pod-product-compliance
Lightning Source LLC
Chambersburg PA
CBHW050929290526
45792CB00002B/946